TO MUM

Jennifer Mary Bromley
Age 5

A gift book written by children for mothers everywhere

Edited by Richard & Helen Exley

EXLEY

To Momtom, who is still the most treasured
and loved mother in the whole wide world..

My mummy smiles

Wendy Sargent

Second edition published 1990

First edition published in Great Britain
in 1976, revised and updated 1981, by

**Exley Publications Ltd,
16 Chalk Hill, Watford,
Herts WD1 4BN, United Kingdom.**

Front cover illustration by Rupa, age 8
Back cover illustration by Adam Hadley, age 5

PRINTING HISTORY
First edition August 1976
Second printing November 1976
Third printing October 1977
Fourth printing August 1978
Fifth printing August 1980
Sixth printing May 1981
Seventh printing August 1981
Eighth printing August 1982
Ninth printing September 1983
Tenth printing April 1984
Eleventh printing June 1986
Twelfth printing October 1986
Thirteenth printing October 1988

Second edition January 1990

Typeset by Brush Off Studios,
    St Albans, Herts.
Printed and bound in Belgium by Proost
    International Book Production, B-2300
    Turnhout.

Mothers, mothers, young and old alike, are still as sweet as ever.

Patricia Lentong

Mothers are incredible. And the people who say so most loudly and clearly are their children. Mums are funny. They have odd habits. They're endearing. But above all, they love their kids irrationally and beyond reason.

The entries in TO MUM are all absolutely genuine – the words, the pictures and the often hilarious spelling mistakes. There is no doubting the message of love that comes across. Again and again children tell of the times their mothers stay up half the night to care for them, of the way they trust their mums, and can confide in them. They also, albeit guiltily, pay tribute to the immense amount of work mothers do for them, which is so often taken for granted.

First published fourteen years ago, and re-printed many, many times, the book has now been re-issued with new pictures and new entries sent in by over fifty schools. We thank all the teachers involved. We hope they've had as much fun collecting the entries as we've had judging them. Children are so creative, so free, so bluntly truthful, that they have a way of getting to the core of things that matter in their lives, stripped of any overlay of pretence.

When TO MUM was first being prepared, our own two children, Dalton and Lincoln, were ten and eleven, and helped with some of the preparation work. Now in their twenties, they both work for the family publishing firm, and it has been great fun to re-issue this charming book, and to see that so few things have really changed in the intervening years. If there's so much love around, there's hope for the world yet!

Richard & Helen Exley

Joanna   Age 8

What is a mother?

Mums are walls which protect their children from the outside world.

Adrian Leto   Age 11

Moms are the people who tell you to put boots on when it is raining, that you need a coat on in a heatwave and that you're still too young to have the radio-control robot that you've wanted since you were three.

William

A mother is a female parent. Somebody to make the beds and wash up. Someone to wake you too early and make you go to bed too early, and some one to see that you *always* do your piano practice.

Susan   Age 11

A mother is a woman who buys you chewing gum and when you have fillings at the dentist she blames you.

Aishling

A mother is a person who lets you stay up late and eat chocolate, to get fat and spoty.

Mark   Age 10

Mother is a housewife, busy all the day,
Shopping in her lunch hour, running all the way.

Linda Parkinson   Age 15

A mum is a person that is always in the right place when you need her.

Claire Bagguely

Mothers put band-aids on your knee when you fall over and come to see you play football when they don't really want to.

David Champneys   Age 10

A mother is supposed to love you and wash boys' smelly socks.

Sally Arthy

Sarah Curry Age 8

7

A mammy puts up with a lot of things like work and children.

Jennifer McGloin   Age 9

A mother is someone some people take for granted.

Paula White   Age 13

A mum is a woman who says "go to bed" and when she says that, you stay very quite and she forgets about you.

Aishling Nolan

A mother is a person who looks after you if you get scared, and if you want your teddy bear.

Elizabeth Bird   Age 8

Mothers drive you ten times round town on Sunday, looking for funny chimneys to report to the teacher.

Timothy Robinson   Age 12

A mum is a person who lets you creep in beside her to watch the horror film (when Dad is out).

Suzanne Pinder   Age 12

Mothers are people who are angry when you're at home and sad when you're away.

Vinay   Age 12

A mum is someone who always asks you to do something when you're just about to do something else.

Genevieve

Moms have to do all the washing because dads throw their smelly socks arond.

Jacqueline   Age 10

A mother is a person who gets married to a man and then she has babies. The baby calls her mother. The baby does the same. She marries when she is older and then she has babies like her mother.

Clara Ortega   Age 8

A mother is a lady who finds a man and they reproduce.

Samantha   Age 9

Moms wash and dry any dirty football uniforms, five minutes before going to school, having only been given them that morning.

Michael Haworth-Maden   Age 12

A mother is not a proper mother if she does not watch a soap two or three times a week.

Andrew   Age 13

A mum is someone who always stands up for you when your dad gets cross with you.

Melissa

Lots of mums put lots of Purfume on. Lots of mums have false theeth and Lots of mums have glasses or false eye brows. Mums where wigs to suffocate the nits.

Philip   Age 10

A mother is someone who sings in the kitchen.

Elisabeth Fenton   Age 12

Mothers are like volcanoes
About muddy puddles on the floor.
Like prehistoric monsters
Like cars screaching
On a wet morning.
Mothers are kind-hearted
Mothers have to be in a hurry
When the door bell goes
The telephone rings
The baby cries
They all start at once.
Some mothers get in a rage
Rushing all over the place
My mother does.

Philip   Age 7

Daniel Griffiths John   Age 8

SOO

Amanda Gray Age 8

10

Multi-purpose mamas

To a toddler, a mother is an explorer, an astronaut, an indian chief, a cowboy ... anything that he thinks of as a game.
To an infant, she is a helper, confider, a comforter, even a protector.
When she listens to a junior she always understands and she is always there to tell worries to.

Alison Bain

A mother is a helper
A finder of lost things
A pocket money giver
An angel without wings. *Laura Dalgleish   Age 8*

My mam is a Jack of all trades and a master of none. She is a nurse when we are ill, a gardener, a chef, cooks super meals, a waitress, a decorator, a chamber-maid, a dressmaker when she makes or knits our clothes, a fruit-picker, a book-keeper when she keeps a budget on her housekeeping, a cleaner, an ironer and most of all she is an Indian (when she's on the warpath). *Julie   Age 13*

God created mother because he could not be present everywhere.

Taniya Sharma   Age 15

Life without them

To all mums everywhere, what would we do without you? Who would do our cleaning and cooking? I certainly wouldn't do it all. What! Wash smelly socks and grubby shirts. Burn my hands in hot, fatty, soapy water, no fear! I'd rather not be born.

Lisa Ollard   Age 13

·If I had not got a mother my bed would not be done and I would be staying up late watching television. I would all ways be spending my money on things that I would not need. My dinners would probably be a tin of Coke and a cold sandwich and no one would be able to take me out in the car. I would have to do all the house work and so I would not have any spare time. At school I would be a little Dracula and so no one would like me. So I am glad to have one.

Michael Jenkins   Age 10

Without a mother the family would always be fighting and there would never be lunch on time.

Jane Moppel   Age 12

If it was not for mothers we would look like a sack of potatoes.

Tony Martin   Age 12

Jacob Thornton   Age 6

What would it be like without a mother?
Have you ever thought?
What would it be like to be an orphan?
How would you like to be bought?

So love you mother all you can,
While you have her now.
She won't be there all your life,
So love her all you can, with all you know how.

Sheryl A. Hartley   Age 12

13

Susan Holliday   Age 7

14

In tribute

It is lovely to have a mam. Mams are lovely people and I am going to be a lovely mother when I grow up. I am going to care for my children like my parents cared for me.

Estelle Moreton

My mommy is very nice in side her and very nice outside. Very nice in side means she is not spitful. She is very kind, and very nice on the outsides means she looked beautiful.

Siobhan   Age 7

The things my mum does for me are uncountible. She has been helping me hours on end ever since I was born.

Mark Lewis   Age 8

I love my mother. She gave birth to me and to her I owe my very being.

Papageorgiou Papakyriacou Zoe   Age 15

She laughs when I laugh, she cries when I cry, she lives when I live. I can't say more about her except that she lives for me and I live for her.

Josephides Panayiota   Age 16

Mothers do not die because they live in the hearts of their children.

Berna Tahmiscioglu   Age 16

Funny old thing

They're really very delightful things, always the best in the world, although quite often very silly things.　　Stephen

Mama does not like maniacs who drive on the road. She also does not like alligators or spiders in her bed.

Sean McDonald　Age 7

Mine is going to have a baby and she told me that she can't smack me till after April.　　Simon　Age 10

My mum says, "Yes dear" when she does not know what I am talking about.　　Tanya　Age 10

The way she worries about my school tests anyone would think she was taking them not me.　　Robert Booth　Age 12

When my mammy talks on the telephone she talks posh.

Hilary　Age 7

My mum likes watching old fogies' things on television, but she's kind – and that is all that matters.　　Rachel　Age 11

My mommy calls me her little tweedy-twer-heart and my sister her goosy.　　Clare Aldridge

Graeme Riddell

A mum doesn't like travelling at 90 m.ph

Ma's like a football. She gets knocked around a bit, but always stays the same shape.

Mark   *Age 11*

Truely most of the time Ma is a lovable old thing, although she has got a knack for breaking plates, cups etc. quite a lot. And it's only very rarely that she trips up when she's carrying the rubbish bin and the result the most untidy room in town.

Jane   Age 13

My mommy gets me nuts because she once put butter in the washing machine instead of washing powder.

Tracey   Age 8

The trouble with mothers is that they don't play games though she gives me a few rotten under arm rolls in the summer after school.

John   *Age 10*

My mom is sometimes silly and sometimes she is telling jokes. I like it being joked it mackes me laugh.

Samantha Doak   Age 7

Mothers are funny things!

Mums are sometimes fussy
about manners and being good;
They're always telling boys and girls
About the things they should

Remember when they're out to tea,
Like manners, – "Do say 'please'
And thank the lady nicely when you
know it's time to leave."

At bath-time there are orders
Like "Don't forget your feet,
Remember dry yourself quite well
And leave the bathroom neat."

But if ever I was judging,
Then with banners all unfurled,
I'd place a crown upon her head
And vote my mum – "Miss World".

John Elliott

Adele Cox   Age 9

Useful people to have around

A mother usually insists that you learn (or try to) a musical instrument.
You are taken to an aged piano teacher, and learn that allegro is a musical term as well as a car.
You learn other things from them too. Nobody lives on Mars, Mass = Density + volume (or the other way round?) and not to put your knife in your mouth. In other words, you start to accumalate a small store of knowledge.
They are useful people to have around.

David Honigmann   Age 9

Putting up with us kids

God didn't have enough arms for keeping kids out of trouble so he invented moms.

Alice Lumpkin   Age 11

If I were my mother, sometimes I would smack me hard.

Diena Lees   Age 11

My mum has weird rules that I have to obey, like having a bath, keeping my bedroom tidy and even having my hair cut.

Christopher Moates   Age 12

She says I'm nicest when I am asleep because I can not say anything wrong.

Richard   Age 12

If I were my mother my children would go to bed at 10 o'clock at night and get up at ten in the morning too. They would not have to take vitamin pills or drink milk of magnesia if they had tummy aches. They would be paid around nothing less than ten per cent tax. The children would be sent to school once a week just to keep up the good education. When it was a birthday I would not insist on inviting someone like Cecilia Pigface to the party.   Katy Berger Age 11

Mothers always nag at you. I think they should be sold at a knockdown price for a sort of trick.   Pablo Age 11

The best think I thought Ma did was having me, but others might not think so.   Tim Tripp Age 12

David Age 7

21

Isn't she a pain . . .

Mothers are the sort of people who, before a western starts in the evening, send you to bed saying how awful it will be and then wake you up saying what a fantastic show it was.

Nicholas

I don't like the way she puts me to bed. When I am wide awake at night, she makes me go to sleep, and when I'm fast asleep in the morning, she makes me get up!

Stephen

The one problem with my mum is she is allways tidying up, if you put anything down and go away for a minuet when you come back to it, it has been tidyed away.

Ian

John   Age 9

Pinickity, pinackity
Lilickety, lilackity
Just like a mother hen
Or even like a mother wren.

It's "Clean your room!"
Or "Don't touch the broom"
"Don't eat too fast.
Make your food last".

P Tucker

Mommy tidys up our rooms and throws my teddy's head away.

Steven

Mothers are funny things really because you never know whether there going to shout at you or not. They say do your bedroom and while your doing your bedroom they tell you to do the stairs and before you know it you have a hole load of jobs to do before your even finished your bedroom. I sometimes wonder where they get them all from.

Heather   Age 10

Mums look after you all the time. Trouble is that she looks after you so much that somtimes it becomes annoying.

Judy   Age 9

I have never been allowed to stay up and see a late night movie yet. My mom says I need sleep so I can work hard at school next day, but I think she sends me to bed so she can watch television in peace.

Billie Mayhook   Age 13

My mother is strange. One minute she is on my side when I'm fighting with my brother then the next minute she's on his side.

Stephen Shaw   Age 10

Sean Charlton
Age 8

Twenty one today

When I ask her how old she is she always says twenty-one. As I have a sister who is twenty-two even dumb old me knows this cannot be right.

Billy Mayhook   Age 13

I think my mother is good looking and so do very many other people. She has dark brown hair and dark brown eyes. You have to give her credit. She is forty-one.

Debbie   Age 13

My mother is a teacher and she knows the answers to most questions except what age she is.

Douglas A. Currie   Age 13

My mum has been thirty-four for the last three years.

Louise

Nicola Breakwell
Age 7

25

Marrina   Age 9

Chatter, chatter

The habit no mum should be without is nattering on the phone; no mother would be complete without it.

Miles Hutchinson   Age 10

One thing mine can't stand is being stood out on the street gabbing away, she would much rather sit down and gab over a cup of coffee.

Dave   Age 14

She is always natting on about her and her sister when she was small, I pretend to listen but I watch TV instead. We just say YEH, YEH, YEH. She soon shuts up.

Timothy

She is always talking and the only time she is quiet is when she is very interested in what's on television and even then she puts in a quick comment. She is also quiet when she is asleep.

Julie   Age 9

James   Age 8

Going out

I think mine is funny because when she plans to go out she has to do her hair, her face and by the time she has finished, it is to late to go out.

Ean   Age 10

Every time Mommy goes out to a dance she puts her false nails on, and she looks ever so funny, and Daddy puts aftershave on, and he smells as well.

Elisabeth   Age 7

My mother powders her face,
Puts lipstick on,
And cover herself in perfume,
That's why my father disowns her at parties.

Sophia   Age 11

My Mummy and daddy going out to the Cinema

Samantha Goulding   Age 8

Andrea Scown   Age 7

29

Mothers make you go to the barbers as though you were going to a dog show.

Peter Wilkinson   Age 11

Volker   Age 14

Learn . . . or else!

I know she always tries to give what she thinks is best for me – even if that is the hard end of the stick.   *Rachel   Age 11*

Mums are vultures that hang over you, telling you that you have to clear the snow or make your bed. They nag at you, giving you lectures on life in general and how to make your bed in particular.   *Peter*

Mothers should not be allowed to start nagging and the best way to stop her is to keep tidy.   *Philippa*

My mom smacks me when I am naughty it hurts me very much but I deserve it.   *Stephen   Age 9*

What ever my mum does wrong I still love her.   *Barry Silverman   Age 10*

Do you know I was born because I wanted to be near my mommy?

Claudia Martinez   Age 8

Ma and me

She is kind and gentle. Sometimes my mother really loves me and she looks at my face and she smiles at me. I go and sit by her.

Balbinder Kaur Kalsi   Age 11

Sometimes Mother is angry. But sometimes it's NOT my fault I get angry and fight back. Mum yells and so do I. But in the night, when everything is still, and I am still awake, I hear mum come in, she whispers that she always has and always will Love me. That is the best part. But she never knows that I am awake, And as sleep overtakes me, I feel, Happy, And Loved....

Vandana Tandon   Age 10

My Mummy some times calls me Funny names and When I do naughty things and I tell the truth she kisses me.

Mark Grundy   Age 6

Alison Baker   Age 7

33

In my mother's arms

My mother always has room for me in her arms. She's never too busy to give our family the special love a mother can only give.

Donna Jauga   Age 9

My mother cares for me. I feel that I've got day and night protection when I'm near her.

Martha van Kees   Age 9

She is the person you can come to for comfort, when all hope is lost, like an old teddy bear with one eye and half an ear.

Patricia Bowie   Age 13

Moms are always busy but never too busy to give you a quick cuddle.

Helen Rankin   Age 9

My mum is nice to sit on. She's nice and soft and bouncey.

Paul Fanneaux   Age 10

Hadas Nahari   Age 9

My mother's hands

These hands lifted me when I was a baby. They dried away the tears when I cried at night or when I was upset. My first food came from her hands. She helped me tie my laces, hold the spoon in my hands, shampooed and bathed me. I remember the sadness I felt when I let go of her hands on my first day at school. Although they may get old and wrinkled I will always remember what those precious hands did for me.

Sean McGilligam

My mother's hands can be soft and hard. They are like smooth silk when she is rubbing my cheeks, and like hot fire when my mother is smacking me for being naughty. They do loving things like combing my hair cleaning my ears and taking care of my clothes. They do sweet things like making waffles and cakes. If I had to give my mother's hands a grade they would get a B+. If it wasn't for the spankings her hands would get a big "A".

Kim Wilkinson

She brushes my hair so it is not tangly.

Teri Cothran 8

The comforter

Mum is very nice in all sorts of ways. When someone's just bashed you in, you can run to her and she'll comfort you.

Simon Fox   *Age 10*

A mom is a person who cares for you and tucks you in at night. When you've made a mistake she says it's quite allright. Someday you will have to grow out of this stage.
She doesn't want to let you out of her big lovable cage. When it's time to leave her and face the big wide world, Always remember: She is the one who cares and she will always shed the most tears.

Jan Menno   *Age 13*

A mother is someone who comforts you. Because she misses you, even for one minute. Because you are her child.

Kristin Thompson   *Age 8*

A mum is someone who always knows when there is something wrong even if you don't tell her.   Lisa Tresa   *Age 14*

Bjarne Kalo   *Age 11*

Cooking

When I come home from school, who would be there to make a delicious, warm chocolate drink and maybe some hot muffins or a quick snack before having a proper dinner. I might have spaghetti bolognaise with a rich luscious pudding, oozing with cream and chocolate sprinkled carefully over the top. Or another night I might have spam and potato with salt and pepper laid over my potato, not forgetting to dribble the tomato sauce over everything. Only a nice, welcoming mother could do that, making things just how you like them.

Lisa Ollard   Age 13

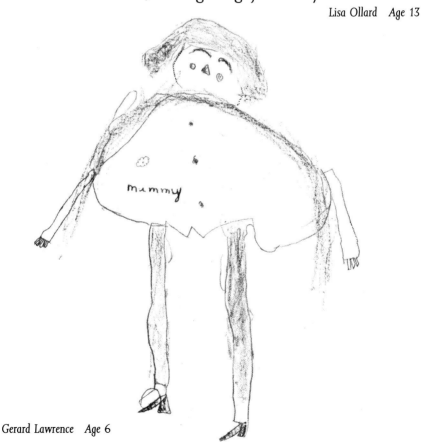

Gerard Lawrence   Age 6

Diets

Daddy each day says "Darling, why don't you eat something. You will be very ill." Ma gets up every morning at 6 o'clock and eats her diet biscuit, which she says contains a whole breakfast of bacon and eggs. Then poor Ma because she has woken up so early, by midday, she gets in a temper! So we all go to a Kentucky Fried Chicken Place, because she is too tired to cook a meal. Well, I don't know, I do hope she stops soon.

Wendy   Age 13

She doesn't have any will-power diet because she isn't very fat and she doesn't have any will-power.

Naral   Age 12

Some nights my mother says that she is going to diet. So she cuts down on potatoes, and sugar in her tea. Then we are sitting watching the television she gets through a box of chocolates! (Or my dad buys some sticky cakes) Then my mom says "I think I'll start my diet tomorrow". I don't think she has ever been on a strict diet in her life but then she would not be the same old cuddly Mom if she was slim.

Jane   Age 12

A mother is quite kind at times because if she's having a crafty eat and you go in she gives you something too.

Mark Dowling   Age 10

My mum is on a diet, a *eating* DIET!

Paul   Age 9

Mum –
Likes antiques
Has even restored some
But hasn't succeeded
With her figure.

Matthew   Age 11

Belgin Akyol
Age 13

39

Like a rose

My mother is medium sized, brown as a berry and as cool as a cucumber. Her hair is red and thick. She has a proud walk, and is as tender as a chicken. A rose is as beautiful as my mother, and she is as fresh as a daisy, and as strong as an ox. When I grow up I would like to be as beautiful as my mother. And have the beautiful ways she has. My mother is more precious than gold.

Carmen Ramnath   Age 11

My mother is the coolest person in the world. Sometimes she looks like a rose and other times she is just a plain daisy. When she is a rose you can imagine that my mom is very nice.

Wanda Michels   Age 11

Mandy Clee   Age 10

40

Abbas   Age 8

She's always there

When you are ill who is always there,
Quietly sitting stroking your hair?
WHO is always waiting for you to come home?
WHO welcomes you with open arms?
WHO never lets you down?
WHO wakes you up with a lovely smile in the morning?
WHO's always ready to help?   *Vivienne Gilbert*

Some mothers' apron strings are never cut, just stretched.
                                          Patricia Sisti   Age 14

When all other friends have deserted you, your mother is
always here.   *Catherine Woodall   Age 14*

Leslie Johnson   Age 6

I Love my mummy

It's Mum!

When things go wrong
And everything you do goes dong!
Who's always there with smile and help
Comfort, love, or if you need it a scalp?
It's MUM.

We mutter and we mumble and chaff
Because Mum says, "No it isn't safe!"
But who knows when to pull the rein
Or give the children their way again?
It's MUM.

And when you come home moping, sad
Or maybe just plain hopping mad
Who knows what's best
To sooth the raging in your breast?
It's MUM.

Ian Laurenson   Age 11

Imagane you are in a stone room with a metal door, metal roof, you are bolted off from the world. Mum is the key. If she is taken away it is nightmares and horrors if she is there it is dreams, treats and love and care if there were no Mums we would be nothing. Mums are the key to the future Mums were put on earth to care and love not to rage and hate. mums help us, guide us and love us. If there were no Mums no us would be there. Mums are to run to for comfort.

Fiona Finch   Age 8

Always a friendly smile,
Always open arms
Willing to help while –
Troubles are at their worst.
The door is always open
To us their children.

Alexandra Hitchings

Elaine Rockley   Age 7

Take good care of her

If you have a mother, give her all your loving care, for you won't know her value, until you see her empty chair.

Mona Fouad El Sakka   Age 16

Mothers deserve a couple of surprises and treats themselves, for all the hard work they do.

Louise Twaite

With all her worrying about her children, Mother seldom has time to worry about herself. There are, of course, adverts and posters telling parents to take care of their children such as:
"A lesson in life" and
"Under your feet is better than under a car."
So, why not have posters saying:
"Take care of your mother, she's valuable" and
"Make sure your parents, Clunk Click Every Trip."

Alpoislan Gumundin

Alison Bain

44

Berrin
Suboiy

45

She's an old softie

A mother is probably the most likley one to give in to you.

Jessica   Age 11

I like my mother best because I don't get smacked so much.

Paul   Age 8

A mum is someone who will ask Dad if you can go on a school.journey, when he has already said no.   Joanne   Age 13

A mother is someone to help you eat your food when you can't eat it all, so it looks like you ate it all.   Teri Burns   Age 11

Even the roughest of mothers are very gentle and kind inside, or else they could not be mothers.   Elaine Wong

If I am naughty I always break it to my mom first.

David   Age 12

Whenever she gets upset she expresses her feelings angrily, but afterwards she is sorry about the harsh things she said and gives us cookies to show us she loves us.   Avery   Age 15

My mum is a bit stupid because every time I ask for something she buy's it me.   Debbie   Age 10

I have a super mother who makes cakes, puts them in the pantry and doesn't notice when I eat them.

Mark Wickham-Jones   Age 13

A mum is sombody who always understands your feelings, special feelings, that only my mother and I will ever know about. A person you'll always remember, the rest of your life. My mum.   Karen Angelini - Age 10

Marilyn Norman   *Age 8*

My mam isn't really a beauty queen, but in my heart she is the prettiest woman in the world.

Ian Age 10

Beautiful in her own way

My mom is as beautiful as anyone can be, well maybe not to everyone but always to me.
Now I don't mean always by looks because you learn all that junk from T.V. and books.
But I mean that she has a beauty inside.   Donna Nitte   age 12

My mother is very kind and when she was younger she was very very pretty. Now she is a bit plump but I like her very very much, she seems to be prettier each day. She doesn't know how to cook very well but when she cooks the dinner it seems to have something special about it. When she makes my bed I think she puts something into it, and I don't awake all night.   Conchita Rey Benayas   Age 10

My mum's, well, she's beautiful in her own way. She's not exactly a beauty queen , but you can't just go and draw a picture of her and say "That's my mother". There's something about her, whether it's her willingness to listen or what I don't know. But I'm glad she's mine.   Daryl Mitchell

A slave to her family

My mom is so busy she has not got any hobbies I suppose her hobbey is cleaning the house.

Craig   Age 9

Be nice to your mother. Don't let her be your work horse, will you?

Donald Ryan   Age 8

I sometimes think that they are bossy and and tempered but when I think about it I realise how hard it is to be a mother. It is make breakfast, wash up, go shopping, cook, wash up, type, meet the school bus, cook, wash, type. I can see why they ask you to wash up or get your own food. I begin to wonder why they ever become mothers in the first place.

Alan   Age 15

Mothers have to wash your hair when they don't want to, and buy you clothes when they don't have any money.

Aaron Sumler

A mum is someone who has to wash faces and count heads when she's ready to go somewhere.

Melonie Dixon   Age 11

A mother is not just a mother, she is a Human Being too.

Barbara Allbritton   Age 11

Who would want to be a mother?

Everyday you clean the house listening to love songs on the radio while you sweep, dust and polish, making our beds, scorching your hands in the washing up, or trying to make the old washing machine work. When all the cleaning's done you can have a rest with a snack and last month's paper which you still have not read. Then there is the shopping and hurry to meet the school bus. Homework comes next. "Mommy how do you do this?" or "Mommy how do you do that?" After supper, Dallas comes on, but of course you have to do the washing up, type more letters, or sew buttons on the school shirts. When she has finished all she is fit for is bed. Perhaps I do not really want to be a mother after all.

Susan

Poor working mothers!

My mother is very patient. She would have to be with five kids, four dogs and two jobs.

Pam Repec   Age 12

My mother gets up between six and half past am and she does some general housework and makes breakfast. At seven she wakes up my two brothers and they all have breakfast. Then Mammy gets the boys ready for school, wakes up Daddy, and at quarter to eight she goes off to work.

Joanna Blake   Age 11

christmas
shopping

Maxine Howitt   Age 10

I wish my mother din't go to work becase I love her.

Danielle   Age 8

A mother is a superwoman who can be in two places at once. She can tie two pairs of sneakers with one hand and stir the pudding with the other. That's what a mom is.

Judy McDonough   Age 10

She does a hell of a job feeding and clothing us!

Paul   Age 13

Mine is the best. She can work, clean, cook and wash and take care of six kids too.

Kellie Harlam   Age 10

A mom is someone who is responsible for cooking and cleaning. Not all mom's do that because a dad can do it too.

Chris   Age 12

They say "A mother's place is in the home", but mine doesn't think so.

Leroy   Age 11

My mum she works so very hard.
She must be near to tears,
Cos' gimie, gimie! More, More!
Are the only words she hears.

She only wants the magic word,
Oh by the way it's PLEASE
She acts just like a servant,
But never asks for fees. .

Susan Harvie   Age 10

Tanita   Age 6

Thank you

My mother is so kind I do not no how to thank her. How can I thank you my Mommy?

David Webb   Age 9

Mother, at every difficult moment in my life I turn to you. You are the only person who can help me whenever I need help, the only person who can make a sacrifice for me. That will be understood only by children who have lost their mothers.

Savva Evangelia   Age 17

Who do you go to when
You're in a mess?
Who do you turn to when
You're in distress?

Who gives you money
When you are flat broke?
Who explains why you're late
When you're out with a bloke?

Of course its your mother
Who else could it be?
Give her a treat sometimes
Perhaps make the tea.

Remember her birthday
And Mother's Day too
You look after her
And she'll look after you!

Debbie Russell   Age 16

Caroline de Silva Age 9

Mother, I will remember your sweet face for ever. Never will I forget anything you did for me.

Savva Evangelia   Age 17

To a very special Mother

This verse is just meant to be, a very special way of saying, "Thank you, Mother".

It isn't easy to express the things I want to say,
For what goes on unnoticed, every single day.
But still you are there, with all your understanding heart
And those never-to-be-forgotten words of advice
Which in the end it brought me joy complete.
So Mom, and all others, a tribute to you,
For you are truly the "Queens" of the world.
(P.S. Don't be a bit worried, Dad, because you aren't so bad.)

Jesse O'Neill   Age 13

Iris Harcel

Temper, temper

On a whole we all love her, except those times when she wallops us.

Robin *Age 12*

She gets mad when all of us done something bad on the same day, and that's the time when you shouldn't bother her too much.

Juanita

Mommys are nice except when they find gum sticking to their carpet.

Michelle *Age 10*

She Sometimes gets mad and once She got So mad that She made us make our own Breakfast.

Mark *Age 9*

Sometimes they can be dangerous like dragging you out of the room by your hair, or the famous clip round the ear.

Paul *Age 9*

My mum is very kind and helpful, but she has her bad times bang crash wallop ouch!

John Age 9

Our mother doesn't often spank us but when she does, she does.

Surjit Age 11

Mom gets up at 7.30 am and begins her routine day of housework, headaches, and yelling.

Mark Age 13

I like my mum very much but when can we get to smack them because they smack us?

Sarah Age 8

57

Sarah Eyule   Age 7½

Lessons in life

A good mother is worth a hundred teachers. The teacher teaches lessons from books while the good mother teaches everything that is useful in life.   Mona Fouad El Sakka   Age 16

When I cried, I remember my mother used to tell me how to overcome sadness. She explained to me that the world is full of evil, and if I didn't learn to be strong I would fail. And when she knew I was strong enough to face reality she began to teach me how to find my way in life. She told me that I must learn to be kind, to be a good friend, and always to be ready to help. But I think the most important thing I learnt was to trust myself. It gave me a lot of confidence. My parents gave me the basic values I needed, and because they taught me how to learn, I learnt all the other things by myself. And for that I thank them and love them.   Michal Arlosoroff   Age 17

And as I grew she shared good times with me. She taught me to be realistic and understanding, she taught me how a mother should be, but most importantly, she taught me how to be a woman.   Debra Duel   Age 15

A home with a good mother is the best of schools. There the child learns the lessons of cheerfulness, patience, self-control and the spirit of service.   Mona Fouad El Sakka   Age 16

Jessica Gould

59

Mother is kind today.
Mother was kind yesterday.
Mother is kind every day.
Mother makes kindness.

Daniel Bajnath   *Age 10*

A watchful eye, a gentle touch,
That happy laugh we love so much,
In every home, there is no other,
Who loves and cares just like a mother.

Gabrielle Smylie   Age 12

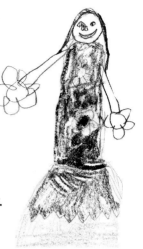

My mother means morning. A beautiful morning.

Abby   Age 7

Mums are really groovey. Helping us when we are sick.
Washing, drying, all the lot. They are hard working ladies busy
here, busy there, busy nearly everywhere.   Ruth Shaw

Mother... That was the first word that I learned when I was
little. And she was the first person I knew and loved.

Berna Tahmiscioglu   Age 16

A mother's worry never ends for her children.

Sheryl A Hartley   Age 12

A mother's smile can give you a little happyness when
your sad.   *Amanda Davey   Age 10*

Mother is a special gift, that God has given to me.

Rookminee Chatergoon   Age 11

"Mum" is the only word that makes everybody all over the
world happy, the symbol of devotion. She gives everything
that she has, sometimes even her life, for her children without
hesitating a moment.   *Hasan Ali Tolgay   Age 17*

Mothers have a heart with a key; they open it and love pours out.

Marcia   Age 9

Claire Mullan   Age 9

A mother is . . .

A mother is someone who has to wash faces and count heads when she's ready to go somewhere. Melonie Dixon Age 11

Mothers are people who sit up worrying about you and when you come home they holler at you. Gary Crees Age 13

A mother is a loving angel. Between her arms you find warmth and love which you can never find anywhere else.
Shahira Yossef Age 16

A mom is when deep down inside there is love.
Aldo A. Gomez Age 7

A mum is a person who cries when you do something bad, and cries even harder when you do something good.
Robin DiBiase Age 14

Lisa Rule Age 9

Sarah Cakebread Age 10

62